The Adventures of Ooga and Zeeta

The 12 Cs: Life Tools to Thrive

Written by Gretchen G. Burman

© Gretchen Burman. 2015.

All Rights Reserved.

ISBN: 978-0-9963275-0-3

Illustrations by Krystle Lemonias
Book layout by Patti Frazee

Published by

South Orange, New Jersey

Contents

Introduction v

Cast of Characters vii

Confident 1
To believe in yourself and your abilities. To believe you will achieve. To know you deserve love and respect. To have a high self-esteem. To be proud of who you are. Inner strength.

Courageous 5
The ability to push through fears and be brave even when you're scared. The ability to handle fear, embarrassment, pain, or anything else you would usually want to avoid. Inner toughness.

Careful 9
Live healthy and safe – stay away from danger, focus on eating healthy and making safety a priority. Take good care of your mind and body. Safety first, safety last, safety always.

Commitment 13
Dream big. Set goals. Work hard. Never give up. Make a promise and keep it.

Centered 17
The ability to make yourself calm and relaxed. The ability to adapt and cope. The ability to manage worries and anxieties. Feeling peace and balance within your mind and body.

Charity 21
Make a positive difference in the world by helping others in need. To give without expecting anything in return.

Comedy 25
To have fun, laugh, smile, and find the joy in life. The ability to laugh at yourself and find humor even in difficult situations.

Cognitive **29**
Training your brain to think and self-talk positively. To focus, brainstorm, and solve problems. To explore your imagination, creativity, and curiosity. To think before you do. Healthy mind.

Choices **35**
To take thoughtful time to make the best possible decisions. To learn from your mistakes and make better future decisions. The ability to decide between two or more options. Understanding you always have a choice.

Compassion **39**
To care about the feelings of another and help them feel better. To treat others as you would like to be treated. To build and sustain healthy friendships. To include others. To have tolerance and accept others as they are.

Communication **43**
Exchanging thoughts and information effectively. Relationship skills. Social skills.

Cherish..**47**
To feel thankful and grateful for what you have. Mindfulness.

Acknowledgment..**51**

"When You Live The 12 Cs" Poem..**55**

Introduction

When I was pregnant with my first daughter I thought a lot about what it meant to be a good parent. How was I going to make sure my child learned the necessary skills to be happy and lead a fulfilled life? I had lots of questions swirling around my head, and then one day I saw a young girl acting extremely inappropriately. How was I going to make sure my daughter didn't behave in that manner!? I thought if I taught my daughter to be confident, she would respect herself and wouldn't behave that way.

I kept thinking and more questions ruminated in my head. How was I going to teach her to be a good person for herself and to care about others? How was I going to teach her to have a high self-esteem and love herself? To dream big and work hard until she reaches her goals? To live with integrity and be kind? To show respect and compassion? To focus on healthy living and safety? To have the guts to go for whatever she wants in life? How was I going to teach her to learn from her mistakes and make better decisions? To make sure she gives back to the community? To know the power of laughter and be able to laugh at herself? How was I going to empower her to be her best?

What were the most important traits to teach her so she was living the answers to all of these questions? I had lots of questions but unfortunately no good answers.

I went to the library to get some parenting books, but I was totally overwhelmed by the number of books and the number of pages of each book. I didn't have time to read 200+ page books. I wanted something simple yet comprehensive. I couldn't find what I was looking for, so I soul searched and identified 12 qualities that I think are fundamental to having a thriving, fulfilled, happy, mindful, authentic, and successful life. That is how The 12 Cs were born.

My goal was to use every opportunity to proactively and reactively teach my daughter these 12 qualities. I knew I couldn't stop the pain of life's ups and downs but I could commit to spending dedicated, uninterrupted time continually teaching her the life tools she would need to know how to stay at her ups longer and get through her downs quicker and easier.

The Adventures of Ooga and Zeeta

After experiencing the benefits of living The 12 Cs with my own family, I wanted to help others who were looking for a consistent way to teach these essential life tools. I wrote *The Adventures of Ooga and Zeeta* children's book to bring The 12 Cs to life and show boys and girls how they too can use these life tools to navigate through real-life situations and be prepared to handle whatever life throws at them today and always. The book contains 12 relatable and memorable stories representing the "Cs", and, together, through the use of fun characters, they teach the power of positive self-talk and positive thinking. These stories provide a sense of hope because children can relate to the specific challenges in the stories, which provides them with inspiration and the knowledge that they are not alone in facing and overcoming life's challenges. Adults are encouraged to spend time reading the book with children and guiding them through the activities and tips for kids that follow each section. The book can also be used as a reference guide to be read over and over again as life issues arise.

Life Tools Program

As I was finishing the book, I kept thinking of ways to assist more adults in helping children learn essential life tools to thrive and succeed. This passion led me to research and collaborate with a team of experts, including mental health professionals, educators, and my eight-year-old daughter. I developed a fun and comprehensive workshop on these 12 life tools in which relatable stories, informative lessons, engaging activities, and thoughtful discussions take place — and everyone leaves with their "life skills toolbox" full of new ideas.

These workshops are intended for:

- Parents and children who want quality, one-on-one dedicated time together to learn these new techniques.
- Educators, counselors, camps, organizations, etc. looking to complement their life skills/character education efforts.
- Anyone interested in learning 12 life tools packaged in a user friendly format to help children pave the way to successfully navigate life's bumpy roads.

The goal of these workshops is for children to learn such life skills while they are young so they are well prepared and know how to handle the ups and downs of life. For more information on the Life Tools Workshop, please visit www.character-u.com.

The 12 Cs help children...

- Believe they deserve love and respect and believe in themselves.
- Believe they can push through their fears.
- Focus on healthy living and safety.
- Take on challenges, work hard, and improve resilience.
- Develop adapting and coping strategies for a peaceful mind and body.
- Help others and make the world better.
- Understand the power of laughter.
- Think positively and think before doing.
- Learn from their mistakes and make better decisions next time.
- Choose healthy relationships and care about the happiness of others.
- Share information effectively and build their relationship and social skills.
- Be mindful and focus on what they do have.
- Live up to their potential and lead happy and thriving lives.

The 12 Cs:

Confident
Courageous
Careful
Commitment
Centered
Charity
Comedy
Cognitive
Choices
Compassion
Communication
Cherish

Cast of Characters

Meet Green Glory and Red Rant

GREEN GLORY

RED RANT

    Green Glory is on one side of your head telling you positive things like, "You can do it," "Keep trying," "Don't give up," and "You deserve love and respect." Green Glory is your positive self-talk and is a life helper!

    Red Rant is on the other side of your head telling you negative things like, "You can't do it," "No one likes you," "You're going to fail," and "You'll never get it, so stop trying." Red Rant is your negative self-talk.

    Green Glory's job is to keep Red Rant from bothering you and bullying your thoughts. Through these teaching stories and activities you will see how Green Glory is Zeeta and Ooga's life helper and how it's always your choice to either listen to Green Glory or Red Rant. Our brain is a muscle. Scientific evidence shows that we can boost areas of our brain that stimulate positive feelings through repetitive positive thinking and activity. This can rewire our brain and strengthen brain areas. Try talking with your Green Glory and it can be your life helper too!

Meet Ooga and Zeeta

    Ooga and Zeeta are brother and sister and their parents teach them The 12 Cs every day, which gives them the life tools to help them through bad days and teaches them how to be their best. They even have posters of The 12 Cs in their kitchen and bedrooms to remind them that The 12 Cs are always there to help.

The Adventures of Ooga and Zeeta

The 12 Cs: Life Tools to Thrive

Confident

*To believe in yourself and your abilities. To believe you will achieve.
To know you deserve love and respect. To have a high self-esteem.
Inner strength. To be proud of who you are.*

Ooga started first grade super excited, but he was soon frustrated because he couldn't read the same level books as his friends. He lost his temper and cried a lot in class. He kept saying he couldn't do anything right.

The teacher realized she needed to help Ooga build his confidence. They created an "I Can" journal, and every time Ooga said he couldn't do something, he had to write three things he could do.

After a few weeks, Ooga realized there were a lot of things he could do. With this new CONFIDENCE, he decided to work really hard until he caught up to his friends in reading. However, he still struggled reading the books and wanted to give up several times. Red Rant kept saying, "Reading is hard and you'll probably never be a good reader, so you might as well give up."

But Green Glory said, "Believe in yourself, keep trying and you'll get it."

Ooga decided to listen to Green Glory.

He continued to try, and eventually it was a lot easier to read. Ooga went from level 2 all the way to level 12, and felt huge pride in his effort and success.

Within one month, Ooga improved his reading skills faster than anyone his teacher had ever seen. Ooga realized that if he believed in himself and worked really hard he could accomplish anything.

Confident Activity

1. Think about something you like that you're embarrassed to tell others. For example, you're embarrassed that you love to read and you think your friends will think you're a nerd.

2. Stand tall with shoulders back while giving yourself eye contact in front of a mirror and practice saying in a confident voice, "I love to read."

3. Write down three things you are good at.

4. Write down three things you like about yourself.

Tips for Kids

- Increase your confidence by building on top of your past successes/experiences.

- Be proud of who you are, just as you are.

- Confident people don't usually get picked on or bullied.

- Say daily positive Green Glory words to keep Red Rant away. For example: "I can do it. I'm stronger and tougher than I think."

- Next time you face a challenge, remember a similar past experience and the positive outcome. Tell yourself, "I did it before so I can do it again."

- Believe that your inner strength is strong enough to ignore Red Rant and listen to Green Glory.

Courageous

The ability to push through fears and be brave even when you're scared. The ability to handle fear, embarrassment, pain, or anything else you would usually want to avoid. Inner toughness.

Zeeta and her family were on vacation in Jamaica. They went to a waterfall where people could safely jump off a tall rock through the waterfall and into the water. Zeeta's father and friends jumped, but Zeeta was too scared. She stayed in the boat with the guide and her mother. When everyone got back into the boat they talked about how much fun they had. Zeeta felt disappointed that she didn't jump.

Zeeta looked for a shorter rock next to the waterfall where she could push through her fears and jump. She found one, but she was still scared. Green Glory said, "You should jump off this rock. You'll feel so proud that you pushed through your fears."

Red Rant said, "You're too much of a scaredy cat to jump."

Zeeta decided to listen to Green Glory. She asked the guide if she could jump off this rock. He said absolutely!

Zeeta climbed onto the rock, took a deep breath, and jumped into the water. Everyone clapped and "whooped!" She was so proud of herself for being COURAGEOUS and brave. She pushed through her fears and was ready for the tall rock on their next vacation.

Courageous Activities

1. Have you ever been in a situation where you were scared but **did** it anyway?
2. How did you feel after?
3. Have you ever been in a situation where you were scared and **did not** do it?
4. How did you feel after?
5. Is there something you want to do but fear is stopping you?
6. What can you do to push through this fear?

Tips for Kids

- If you want to overcome something, then use your courage and push through your fears.

- Being courageous doesn't mean you aren't scared. It means you are scared, but push through your fears and do it anyway.

- It's important to use your courage to stand up for yourself and others.

- Ignore Red Rant, who puts doubt in your mind. Instead, listen to Green Glory who says, "You can do it!"

Careful

Live healthy and safe – stay away from danger, focus on eating healthy, and making safety a priority. Take good care of your mind and body. Safety first, safety last, safety always.

It was Zeeta's first day of school and time for recess. She brought out a ball and accidently kicked it into the street. As she stood on the curb watching the ball roll down the street, she heard Green Glory say, "Listen to the recess monitor and don't go into the street."

But Red Rant said, "Don't listen to the recess monitor. Run, go get the ball!"

Zeeta started taking a step into the street, but saw a big truck coming around the corner and remembered she wasn't being safe. She decided to listen to Green Glory.

The recess monitor got the ball and explained to Zeeta that she needed to be more CAREFUL.

Recess was over and Zeeta learned a very good lesson about safety. Never go into the street without an adult. Zeeta shared her safety learnings with the class. Everyone was happy that she was okay and glad she shared what had happened so they could learn from it.

The next day at recess her friends were playing with the ball and it kept rolling into the street. Zeeta reminded her friends to be careful and not go into the street.

Instead, they found a solution to their problem: They moved their game farther away from the street so the ball wouldn't roll off the playground. No one's ball ever went into the street again.

Careful Activity

1. Think of a time when you should be careful.

2. Name two things you do to stay safe.

3. Name five healthy foods you can eat all of the time.

Tips to Kids

- The rest of The 12 Cs don't mean anything if you aren't safe.

- Do all that you can to stay healthy by eating balanced foods and exercising.

- Always be aware of your surroundings.

- It's up to you whether you listen to Green Glory, who keeps you safe, or Red Rant, who puts you in danger.

Commitment

Dream big. Set goals. Work hard. Never give up. Make a promise and keep it.

There was a fundraiser announced at Zeeta's school for the American Heart Association to help sick children. That night Zeeta asked her parents to help make a list of family and friends she could call to ask for money for this important charity.

Once the list was complete Zeeta was ready to start calling. She called a few people and they said no. Zeeta was disappointed. Red Rant said, "People just aren't interested in donating so you should quit."

But then Green Glory said, "Don't give up. Keep calling people until you reach your goal."

Zeeta decided to listen to Green Glory.

She practiced in front of a mirror what to say to improve her speech. She even added information to better explain the purpose of the charity. She continued calling family and friends with a positive, can-do attitude. Several people said yes and were happy to donate. Her Uncle Harold even donated $25!

Zeeta was so proud of herself that she set a goal, worked hard, and didn't give up. She achieved her goal of raising $250. Her COMMITMENT helped sick children and that made Zeeta feel happy.

Commitment Activity

1. Think of a time when you worked really hard.
2. How did you feel after?
3. Do you have a current goal you want to complete?
4. What is your plan to achieve your goal?

Tips for Kids

- Commitment is about working hard and never giving up. It's not about being smart.

- Do what you say you're going to do.

- If at first you don't succeed, try, try again.

- Set goals and don't stop until you reach them, no matter how long it takes.

- Failure is not the end, failure is an opportunity to learn and grow.

- It's your choice to listen to Green Glory and stay committed, or listen to Red Rant and give up.

Centered

The ability to make yourself calm and relaxed. The ability to adapt and cope. The ability to manage worries and anxieties. Feeling peace and balance within your mind and body.

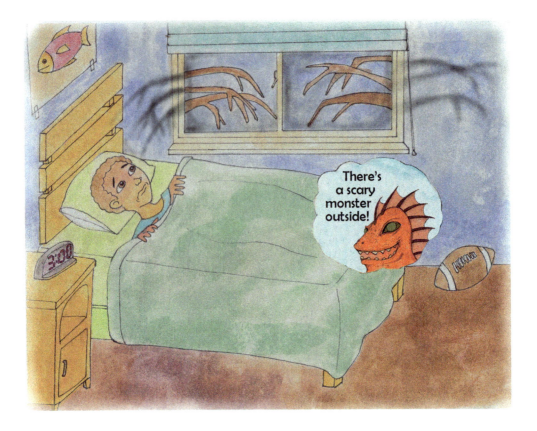

It was 3:00 a.m. and Ooga frantically awoke from a deep sleep because he thought he heard a monster. He went into his parents' bedroom crying and wanted to sleep with them. They encouraged him to go back to his room and read, draw, or watch his goldfish swimming, but he had to stay in his room. Ooga tried to do all of those things, but none of it was working.

Just then he thought he saw the claws of a monster. That was scary enough, but then he heard the claws knocking on the window. Ooga was really scared to be alone. Green Glory said, "You're safe! It's just some branches in the wind brushing against your window outside."

Red Rant said, "I am real and I am going to keep scaring you so you can't sleep!"

Ooga decided to listen to Green Glory.

He realized he needed to get CENTERED. He took several deep breaths and visualized himself at the beach playing in the sand. He wrote in his journal to take his mind off the giant, black claw hands. Within a few minutes, Ooga was asleep and happily dreaming.

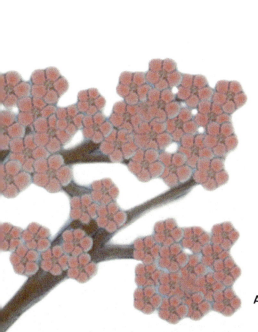

Centered Activity

1. Close your eyes and take three long, deep breaths.

    - three seconds breathing in through your nose
    - three seconds holding your breath
    - five seconds breathing out through your mouth

2. Tighten your entire body from your head to your toes for five seconds and then release. (Think about your body as being a dry piece of spaghetti while you tighten and then release it into a wet, flexible piece of spaghetti.)

3. How do you feel?

Tips for Kids

- Breathe. Breathe. Breathe. It will help you feel calmer.

- You may not have control over all situations, but you always have control of how you handle your feelings and how you react.

- When you're calm, you make better choices.

- It's your choice to ask Green Glory to help you relax and let it go.

Charity

*Make a positive difference in the world by helping others in need.
To give without expecting anything in return.*

Zeeta had begged her parents for two years to take her to the American Girl store in New York City to buy her first doll and outfit. She was so excited! As they walked around the store, Zeeta saw the Doll Hair Salon and also decided she really wanted to get her doll's hair styled. Zeeta's mom felt there were better ways to spend their money. She reminded Zeeta that there were children that didn't have enough money for food. She gave her a choice – get her doll's hair styled or give the money to charity. Red Rant said, "This small amount of money won't really make a difference and won't help anyone. You should get your doll's hair done."

Green Glory said, "You should give the money to charity because any amount of money is better than zero. It's the right thing to do."

As Zeeta stood there watching other girls getting their dolls' hair done, she decided to listen to Green Glory! Zeeta and her parents talked and chose to donate the money to a local CHARITY that feed hungry children.

This made both Zeeta and her parents feel good that they would help feed hungry tummies. They happily walked out of the store with Zeeta's brand new doll and outfit.

Charity Activity

1. Think of a time when you gave back to your community or helped another in need.

2. How did you feel after?

3. Brainstorm at least three ways for you to give back to your community.

4. Pick one and really try to do it.

Tips for Kids

- It's very important to give back to your community and help those in need.

- You alone can make a difference in the world.

- You can read to sick people, raise money, write thank you letters to our military service men and women, or simply help someone carry a bag.

- It feels good to help another in need.

- It's up to you to spread Green Glory's help.

Comedy

To have fun, laugh, smile, and find the joy in life. The ability to laugh at yourself and find humor even in difficult situations.

Ooga met his very first friend Lilly when he was just two weeks old. They have been great friends ever since. One day, Lilly's family came over for a barbecue and they played and had so much fun together. They decided to do a rock concert for their parents and it went great and everyone clapped and cheered.

After the rock concert the children didn't want the fun to end. They wanted to turn on dance music and play a game of freeze dance with their parents. Red Rant said, "Your parents will never want to dance so don't bother asking." Green Glory said, "Your parents are super fun, so of course they'll want to play freeze dance."

They listened to Green Glory and easily pulled their parents out of their chairs and everyone immediately started dancing and didn't stop until they were out of breath. It was so much fun that everyone lost track of time.

The play date was so long that they had lunch and dinner together while playing, laughing, and having a blast. They don't get to see each other very often because they live in different towns now, but when they do get together it's like a party. They know how important it is to have laughter and COMEDY in their lives and look forward to their next play date!

Comedy Activity

1. Think of a time you laughed so hard your cheeks hurt.

2. Who makes you laugh? Try to spend more time with them.

3. Set up a family comedy night once a week. Play games, sing, dance, or whatever makes the family feel happy.

Tips for Kids

- It's healthy to laugh, so do it often.

- Laughter releases stress just as well as tears—and it's a lot more fun.

- Surround yourself with positive people who make you smile and laugh.

- Try to find humor every day, even during tough times.

- Laugh at yourself and try not to take yourself too seriously.

- Smile; it will brighten your day and someone else's day.

- Next time you are upset ask Green Glory to remind you of something funny. Distract yourself with humor.

Cognitive

Training your brain to think and self-talk positively. To focus, brainstorm, and solve problems. To explore your imagination, creativity, and curiosity. To think before you do. Healthy mind.

Zeeta worked very hard to write her short story and today was the big day for her to read it to her class in school. She was so nervous her stomach hurt, as if there were five golf balls bashing together. She thought, "Maybe I shouldn't read my story in class. My story is boring and my classmates won't like it. I bet it's not too late to cancel."

Zeeta told her teacher, Ms. Jo, how she was feeling. Ms. Jo thought that other kids may be feeling the same way so she read a story with the class.

> Red Rant says to the nervous student, "I don't know why you are reading your story. Everyone knows your stories are boring and not good enough."
>
> The nervous student is sad. She is surprised and upset that Red Rant talked to her that way. She couldn't believe Red Rant didn't believe in her and didn't cheer her on.
>
> Then Green Glory says to the nervous student, "Good luck today when you read your story. I know you're going to do great, because it is such an amazing story. I bet you feel really proud of it."
>
> The nervous student is happy. She smiles and is grateful that her good friend Green Glory believes in her and cheers her on.

Then Ms. Jo asks the class, "Which friend would you want to be around? Red Rant or Green Glory?" Isn't it obvious the class answered, *we want to be around Green Glory!* The class didn't understand why Red Rant was talking so mean.

Ms. Jo explained that Red Rant is YOU talking negatively to yourself. This is what you sound like when you say "I can't do it" or "I'm terrible" or anything that puts yourself down when you talk negatively about yourself. She explained that we all have a choice to talk to ourselves positively like Green Glory or negatively like Red Rant. If you choose to listen to negative Red Rant then you are choosing to be around someone who is always finding something wrong with you and tearing you down and making you feel bad.

Zeeta's Red Rant was bullying her thoughts and talking negatively, but after hearing Ms. Jo's story Zeeta decided to use her COGNITIVE skills and listen to Green Glory. She read her story with confidence. She had worked so hard on her story and didn't want her fears or worries to stop her from reading to the class. Zeeta read her story and everyone clapped and told her they couldn't wait to hear her next one.

Cognitive Activity

1. Do you talk to yourself?
2. Are your thoughts mostly positive or negative?
3. Practice telling Red Rant to be quiet and to stop bullying your thoughts.
4. Think of a time you fixed a problem using your positive Green Glory self-talk.

Tips for Kids

- There are two sides to your self-talk.
    - Green Glory (positive self-talk) and Red Rant (negative self-talk).
    - Red Rant may say, "I don't want to try because I will probably fail."
    - Green Glory may say, "I'm not sure I can do it now, but I will keep trying until I can do it."

- Most challenges can be solved if you talk it through with Green Glory.

- Think before you do.

- Explore and appreciate your imagination, creativity, and curiosity.

- Understand the power of your thoughts and practice listening to Green Glory.

Choices

To take thoughtful time to make the best possible decisions. To learn from your mistakes and make better future decisions. The ability to decide between two or more options. Understanding you always have a choice.

It was the middle of the school year and Ooga's teacher, Ms. Lewis, assigned a new project. At the end of the day, each student would think about the school day and grade their behavior.

Ooga had a bad day and was scolded by Ms. Lewis a few times for being a clown and for talking when he should have been listening. At the end of the day, Ooga gave himself a yellow, which means "needs to improve." He was very disappointed and told his teacher he hated himself.

Ms. Lewis agreed with Ooga's grade, because his behavior wasn't good throughout the day. Ooga stomped away and stood in the corner by himself. Red Rant said, "It is Ms. Lewis's fault since she didn't listen to me."

While Ooga stood there, Green Glory said, "You didn't behave well today, but you have a choice of how you behave tomorrow. This is not the end of the world, just do better tomorrow."

Ooga decided to listen to Green Glory.

Ooga apologized to Ms. Lewis for misbehaving and told her he would make a different CHOICE tomorrow and listen. Ms. Lewis appreciated this so much. "There's nothing you can do about the past," Ms. Lewis said. "However, you have all the power to make a different choice now and in the future."

Choices Activity

1. Think of a situation when you made the wrong choice.
2. What did you learn from your wrong choice?
3. What choice will you make next time?

Tips for Kids

- If you do make a wrong choice, learn from it, forgive yourself, and focus on making a better choice next time.

- You always have a choice.

- If you don't know what choice to make, take your time and review your options before making your decision.

- You always make the choice between listening to Green Glory or Red Rant.

Compassion

To care about the feelings of another and help them feel better. To treat others as you would like to be treated. To build and sustain healthy friendships. To include others. To have tolerance and accept others as they are.

Zeeta had a play date at her good friend Tia's house. They were having a great time playing with their dolls until Tia got sad and quiet. Zeeta asked her what was wrong. Tia was embarrassed to say what she was feeling, but Zeeta told her she wanted to help.

Tia told Zeeta that she felt like no one in class liked her. Tia's Red Rant was saying to her, "Your classmates only play with you because the teacher makes them. They don't really like you."

Zeeta gave Tia a big hug. She felt so bad that Tia felt this way.

Zeeta told Tia that sometimes she feels like no one likes her either. She explained to Tia that she chooses to listen to her Green Glory and tells Red Rant to go away when she is feeling down. Tia decided she would listen to her own Green Glory who said, "You have a lot of great friends who care about you."

Zeeta felt a lot of COMPASSION toward Tia. At the end of the play date, they hugged again and Tia thanked Zeeta for being such a great friend. Zeeta was happy that Tia was happy.

Compassion Activity

1. Think of a time when you helped someone feel better.

2. How did it make you feel?

3. Think of at least one nice thing you can do to help someone else feel better. For example, write a get-well card to a friend whose mother is sick, hold the door open for someone, or stand up for someone.

4. Next time you see someone sitting or playing alone, ask them to join you.

Tips for Kids

- Care about other people's happiness.

- If people spent more time thinking of others, we would have more kindness and the world would be a better place.

- Compassionate people have stronger friendships.

- Surround yourself with compassionate people who care about your happiness.

- You can make a difference in someone's day and make their Red Rant go away.

Communication

*Exchanging thoughts and information effectively.
Relationship skills. Social skills.*

One day at recess, Zeeta's best friend Rebecca was playing the game Sorry with another girl. Zeeta asked Rebecca if she could play too. Rebecca told Zeeta she couldn't play because she didn't know how to play the game.

Zeeta felt angry and sad that her best friend didn't want to play with her. Zeeta told Rebecca that they weren't friends anymore and she stomped away. Rebecca didn't understand why Zeeta was upset, but she continued to play the game with the other girl.

That night, Zeeta sat in bed thinking about her "fight" with Rebecca. Green Glory said, "You should talk to Rebecca tomorrow and share your feelings with her."

Then Red Rant said, "She's not your friend; she must not like you if she doesn't want to play with you."

Zeeta already missed her friend and decided to listen to Green Glory.

The next day, Zeeta told Rebecca that she was sad and her feelings were hurt because Rebecca didn't want to play with her. Rebecca listened like a good friend. She didn't realize how much she upset Zeeta and told her she was really sorry.

Rebecca was so happy Zeeta COMMUNICATED her feelings, because she would never want to hurt her best friend. Rebecca taught Zeeta the game and now they play together at recess all the time.

Communication Activity

Role play activity

First role play:

Red Rant: You're a freckle baby.

Green Glory: Stooppp!

Red Rant: What's wrong freckle baby?

Green Glory: You're not my friend anymore!

Second role play:

Red Rant: You're a freckle baby.

Green Glory: Please stop calling me freckle baby because it hurts my feelings.

Red Rant: I'm sorry. I didn't realize I was upsetting you. I won't say it again.

Green Glory: Thank you.

1. Which role play had clear communication?
2. Why was it clear communication?

Tips for Kids

- Good communication can keep smaller problems from becoming bigger problems.

- Good communication helps build and keep friendships.

- You have the power to communicate Green Glory's positive talk or Red Rant's negative talk.

- Non-verbal body language and tone of voice can change the meaning of what you are trying to say.

Cherish

To feel thankful and grateful for what you have. Mindfulness.

Zeeta wanted a sister or brother sooo badly. She kept telling her parents she would be a great big sister and help out all the time. Her parents said when the time was right they would welcome a new baby. Zeeta waited and waited and waited. It seemed like forever, but finally it happened.

Zeeta's mother showed her a picture of the tiny baby in her tummy. Zeeta was thrilled! They surprised her dad that night with the amazing news. They put Zeeta's baby dolls all over the kitchen and had cups of apple juice ready to make a toast. When her dad got home, they all hugged, and a few happy tears even rolled down their cheeks.

When the baby arrived Zeeta wanted to hold him all the time. However, after a few weeks Zeeta was totally over all the crying and smelly diapers. She wanted peace and quiet.

Zeeta went to bed feeling like she didn't want a brother anymore.

Green Glory said, "Try to be patient. The baby will grow up soon and you'll have so much fun together."

Red Rant said, "Hit him so he'll stop crying."

Zeeta decided to listen to Green Glory.

After a good night's sleep, Zeeta felt better. She CHERISHED being a big sister and would try to remember Green Glory's advice next time the baby cried or pulled Zeeta's hair.

Cherish Activity

1. Think of one thing you are grateful for.

2. Create a Cherish Journal and write what you are grateful for one to two times per week.

3. How did you feel after the week of writing in your Cherish Journal?

Tips for Kids

- Write down what you are grateful for and it will remind you of all the good you have in your life and that will make you happier.

- Focus on appreciating what you do have and spend less time thinking about what you don't have.

- Thank Green Glory for protecting you from Red Rant.

Acknowledgment

I want to thank so many people for helping me make *The Adventures of Ooga and Zeeta* book a reality. I created The 12 Cs eight years ago and never imagined they would lead me to write a book and develop a workshop. With the encouragement, support, and kindness of many, I am thrilled that my passion and belief in The 12 Cs can now reach others so they can learn these life skills that I think are so important to living the best possible life. I consulted with family, friends, and experts for research, inspiration, and content validation. I owe my eternal gratitude for the kindness and generosity of the many people who either helped me with the book and/or the Life Tools Workshop.

First, I want to thank my entire family for listening, supporting, encouraging, advising, and helping me overall through this awesome process.

To my amazing, kind, generous, loving, and supportive daughter, Payton, for being my inspiration and muse. She is credited for all of the characters' creation, design, and personality and I am so grateful for her imagination, which brought them to life forever. I practiced my curriculum and activities with her MANY times and appreciatively took her advice and recommendations, which dramatically improved my program. I literally could not have done this book or workshop without her! I can never thank her enough for her endless support, dedication, and loving encouragement. She is my biggest fan and I love her more than I ever thought possible.

I want to thank my other daughter Morgan for making me laugh whenever I needed a break and for allowing me to keep my passion alive. She is only two years old, but I look forward to teaching and living The 12 Cs with her through this book. I am so grateful she is in my life.

Next, I want to lovingly thank my husband Darren, who listened to me read my stories and curriculum OVER and OVER again. He didn't always know how to help me, but being there was what I really needed and he very much accomplished this. I am so appreciative of his patience, love, and support. I am a lucky woman to have such a wonderful and encouraging husband.

To my mother and father, Sandee and Sandy Geschmay, who listened to me with pride, love, and support as The 12 Cs came to life. They always made me feel like I could accomplish anything I set my mind to. And an extra special thank you to my mother for reviewing my 100 or possibly more variations of my flyer, tag line, and company name with an encouraging and loving attitude. I felt stuck so many times and her helpful ideas helped me move forward.

To my sister, Sonja Linn, I want to thank her for reviewing my curriculum and activities to ensure my content can help the most people. I am so appreciative that she shared her experience and expertise to help me, and ultimately the children who read the book and/or participate in my workshop.

To Emily Burman and Donny Pope, I want to thank them for caring about my passion, offering their guidance, and supporting me during this adventure. They have been there since the beginning and have seen The 12 Cs evolve and I am grateful for their listening ear. And an extra thank you to Emily who was so helpful with my final edits when I couldn't see straight anymore.

There have been so many other people who have supported me and gone out of their way to help. It truly has been a heart-warming experience.

I want to thank Jill Pope for encouraging me to bring The 12 Cs to life. She was the first person outside my immediate family who loved the concept and felt children could really benefit by being taught these life tools. She shared The 12 Cs with her co-workers and they loved the idea as well. This positive reinforcement helped push me into action and now I am a proud and hopeful author that my book and workshop can help many children.

To Jamie Pope, who helped me brainstorm at the beginning of my journey and pointed me in the right direction. She introduced me to the idea of character education and encouraged me to pursue bringing my program into schools.

Rebecca Fausel is a dear friend who generously gave me her time and helped me with the curriculum, activities, and so much more. She supported me through my ups and downs and has been a great friend.

Robyn Ferrari is a friend who read my Character U Facebook page, visited my website, and loved my program and concept. She is responsible for helping me get my first workshop into a school. I hope I can help her as much as she's helped and believed in me.

Kirsten Angel is a former teacher I met at a networking event who understood my struggles and generously offered to help me with her time and expertise. Not only did she help me with my workshop content but she "fixed" my flyer. By this I mean she redesigned my flyer, because after 100 versions my messaging and look still wasn't right. I was too close to my work and she recognized this and saved the day. She got me through a "stuck" time and I am so grateful for her gift of time and generosity to help me. She even got her husband to help me with some final editing so I thank him for his time and expertise as well.

To my BABBs, Kanani Briggs, Amy Naim, Mallika Malhotra, Nureed Saeed, Uma Stewart, Mona Malhotra and Elaine Wang Yu, thank you for listening and helping me with your advice and insight into growing my business. You are all impressive entrepreneurs and I feel so blessed to be part of this group.

There are so many other amazing people who helped along the way and I'll list them by name, because this acknowledgement would be longer than the book if I explained how each person helped me: Saul Simon, Julie Coraggio, Teresa Bernstein, Brittany Fitzgerald, Elizabeth Payne, Melanie Girton, Keri Siry, Nerissa Aschoff, Danielle Mann, Katie Gaffney, Andrea Garrido, Kristen Mitchell, Liza Carey, Martina Remy, Rachel Goldberg, Jennifer Kantor, Tracy Freeman, Vanessa Parvin, Pam Yudko, and Marietta Zacker. There are even more people that helped and I thank all of those who cared and listened. I will forever cherish these relationships for their support, advice, and encouragement.

I also want to thank my very talented illustrator, Krystle Lemonias, who was a pleasure to work with. She took my stories on paper and brought them to life. I can't thank her enough for bringing my daughter's visions of Ooga, Zeeta, Green Glory, and Red Rant to life.

In addition, I want to thank my copy editor and layout designer, Patti Frazee, who did much more than her official job. She was a partner and consultant in this overwhelming process. I needed her expertise and she generously gave it to me.

It has taken a village of amazingly kind and supportive people to get my book and workshop completed. Both have been a labor of love, and I am so happy to get them introduced to children so they can learn these 12 life tools in a simple and memorable way to help them thrive. Everyone has ups and downs and that is part of growing up, but my goal of The 12 Cs is to help children learn how to stay at their ups longer and get through their downs quicker and easier.

When you live the 12 Cs you will...

1. Believe in yourself, be **CONFIDENT** and know you are worth it.
2. Push through your fears and be **COURAGEOUS**.
3. Be **CAREFUL** because you know the importance of safety and healthy living.
4. Focus on **COMMUNICATION** to be a good listener and be understood.
5. Keep your **COMMITMENTS**, work hard and never give up.
6. Show your **COMPASSION** and help others feel better.
7. **CHERISH** what you have.
8. Include **COMEDY** and laughter in your life.
9. Adapt, cope and be **CENTERED** to live a balanced and peaceful life.
10. Know you have **CHOICES** and learn from your mistakes.
11. Give back to the community through **CHARITY**.
12. Use your **COGNITIVE** skills to look at life positively.

CPSIA information can be obtained
at www.ICGtesting.com
Printed in the USA
LVOW06s0028091117
555589LV00004B/40/P